SCOTT JOPLIN RAGTIME
CLASSICS
for Bb CLARINET and PIANO
Arranged by
MARCEL G. FRANK

Contents

EDWARD B. MARKS MUSIC COMPANY

Exclusively Distributed By
HAL•LEONARD CORPORATION
7777 W. BLUEMOUND RD. P.O. BOX 13819 MILWAUKEE, WI 53213

2

THE ENTERTAINER
A RAG TIME TWO STEP
For B♭ Clarinet Solo and Piano

B♭ Clarinet

by SCOTT JOPLIN
Arranged by Marcel G. Frank

SCOTT JOPLIN'S NEW RAG
For B♭ Clarinet Solo and Piano

4

B♭ Clarinet

by SCOTT JOPLIN
Arranged by Marcel G. Frank

6

THE EASY WINNERS
A RAG TIME TWO STEP
For B♭ Clarinet Solo and Piano

by SCOTT JOPLIN
Arranged by Marcel G. Frank

B♭ Clarinet

THE ENTERTAINER

A RAG TIME TWO STEP

For B♭ Clarinet Solo and Piano

by SCOTT JOPLIN
Arranged by Marcel G. Frank

15730-20

4

SCOTT JOPLIN'S NEW RAG
For B♭ Clarinet Solo and Piano

by SCOTT JOPLIN
Arranged by Marcel G. Frank

THE EASY WINNERS
A RAG TIME TWO STEP
For B♭ Clarinet Solo and Piano

by SCOTT JOPLIN
Arranged by Marcel G. Frank

15730-20

PLEASANT MOMENTS
RAG TIME WALTZ
For B♭ Clarinet Solo and Piano

by SCOTT JOPLIN
Arranged by Marcel G. Frank

16

15730-20

THE CASCADES

A RAG
For B♭ Clarinet Solo and Piano

by SCOTT JOPLIN
Arranged by Marcel G. Frank

15730-20

15730-20

PLEASANT MOMENTS
RAG TIME WALTZ
For B♭ Clarinet Solo and Piano

by SCOTT JOPLIN
Arranged by Marcel G. Frank

B♭ Clarinet

THE CASCADES
A RAG
For B♭ Clarinet Solo and Piano

by SCOTT JOPLIN
Arranged by Marcel G. Frank

B♭ Clarinet